THE POWER OF PRINT
(IN MARKETING)

THE POWER OF PRINT
(IN MARKETING)

USING PRINT TO BOLSTER A MULTI-TOUCH MARKETING CAMPAIGN

BY CYNDIE SHAFFSTALL

       2/24/15

THE POWER OF PRINT (IN MARKETING)
How print bolsters a multi-touch marketing campaign.

BY CYNDIE SHAFFSTALL

ISBN-13: 978-1508626183

ISBN-10: 1508626189

C Shaffstall & Son, LLC DBA Spider Trainers

PO Box 280487

Lakewood CO 80228

303 862 8951

http://www.spidertrainers.com

To report errors, please send an email to spidertrainer@spidertrainers.com

ALSO BY CYNDIE SHAFFSTALL

FICTION

Seed Money

The Scribe

NONFICTION

Small-business Guide to Winning at Web Marketing

Camera-Ready with QuarkXPress (originally released as
QuarkXPress: Making the Most of Your Negative Experiences)

NONFICTION COAUTHOR

QuarkXPress 8: production tricks and experts' tips

Adobe Web Design & Publishing Unleashed   *Using the Macintosh*

Using PowerPoint 4 (Mac & Windows)   *Using QuarkXPress*

Using CorelDRAW! 5   *Using ClarisWorks 2.1*

EBOOKS

Automated Email Marketing   *Email Automation: Blast, Drip, & Nurture*

Celebrate Unsubscribes   *Great Big Book of Things Marketers Say*

Great Big Book of Things Marketers Count   *Marketing Metrics*

Prospects, Leads, & Subscribers   *Repurpose Your Content*

Targeted Landing Pages   *The CRM Cycle*

The Power of Print (in Marketing)   *Using LinkedIn as a B2B Marketing Machine*

White Paper Tips

          2/24/15

PREFACE

Marketing automation has been shown to increase qualified leads for businesses by as much as 451%. As experts in drip and nurture marketing, Spider Trainers is chosen by companies to amplify lead and demand generation while setting standards for design, development, and deployment.

Our ebooks are designed to help you get started, and while we may be guilty of giving too much information, we know that the empowered and informed client is the successful client. We hope this ebook does that for you.

 2/24/15

CONNECT AND GET COOL AND FREE STUFF

Admittedly, it's just a simple newsletter—not unlike the other dozen already coming to your inbox—but it is chock full of tidbits and special considerations: you'll be put at the top of the list for notices about my upcoming and new releases, you might win free copies of my novels or business books, you'll very probably get preferred discounts, and—the best part—you'll be a member of a community of people who love to read.

Click here to join my preferred readers' list.

In addition to the usual stuff, I'll send out early reveals, talk about authors I enjoy reading, and in general, keep you up to date about my world of fiction and nonfiction.

Please join now and stay in touch.

—*Cyndie Shaffstall*

YOU SHOULD READ THIS IF:

- You want to improve the conversion rate of your marketing campaigns.

- You are looking for marketing vehicle ideas.

- You've heard of multi-touch marketing, but don't see how it can fit into your marketing plans.

- You want to learn to deploy a successful multi-touch marketing campaign.

- You need creative services help in developing marketing campaigns.

TAGS

- Marketing

- Marketing automation

- Automated marketing

- Drip marketing

- Nurture marketing

- Multi-touch marketing

- Just-in-time marketing

- Email marketing

- Auto-responders

- Direct mail

- Print marketing

- Direct marketing

TABLE OF CONTENTS

INTRODUCTION

Printers the world over are feeling the pinch of being known for, well… print.

Listening to the buzz, print does seem to be at risk. We hear of the demise of yet another newspaper nearly weekly, and mobile devices are churning off production lines at an alarming rate. Despite the reports schoolbooks, newspapers, and coupons are going the way of the dodo bird, the fact is that survey after survey finds people simply prefer tangible printed products. In many cases, direct mail still out-performs email and with fewer marketers using direct mail, the mailbox is a much quieter place than the inbox.

The demise of print may be imminent—who can say for sure—but the demise is not today.

For us marketers, we look to our printers with a focus on communication, not just on producing print. We need the lift print provides—and that is the premise of multi-touch marketing. An approach where it's not about choosing print over electronic, it's about supporting your message with appropriate vehicles.

When offline communication—print—is combined with online communication—email and web—both sides benefit, and, of course, the customer too.

Online analytics and tracking are extended to the print vehicles and digital vehicles are bolstered by the tactile preference people have for print. Most importantly, the entire campaign benefits from the simultaneous deployment of multiple vehicles with the same message.

In this ebook, we look at print with excitement. It is a time-honored format that is of the earth, sustainable, and just plain feels good. It is the power of multi-touch marketing. The Power of Print.

Each percentage point of paper recovery represents roughly 800,000 tons of fiber, enough to fill more than 7,500 railroad cars.

— Institute of Scrap Recycling Industries

         2/24/15

CHAPTER 1: ADDING THE POWER OF PRINT

As an offline- and online-marketing services provider, Spider Trainers knows firsthand the power of print when added to any online marketing campaign. In this ebook, we'll load you up with ideas for creating a multi-touch marketing campaign where print is the pivotal moment—and when the recipient says, "WOW!"

When we talk with our clients about including print in the campaigns we build, we often hear objections about how print is old school, cuts down trees, is too expensive, and all sorts of other misguided assumptions. If you're in that camp, consider these stats:

- 92% younger, digitally savvy shoppers prefer weekly direct mail and identify these vehicles as the most-significant information channels.

- 85% of consumers sort through and read selected pieces of mail every day.

- 73% of consumers prefer mail for receiving new product announcements or offers from companies with whom they do business, as compared to 18% from email.

- 70% of customers renew a business relationship because of a direct-mail promotion.

- 69% of shoppers rely weekly on newspapers.

- 67% of shoppers rely weekly on direct mail for sales and product information.

- 40% of customers are driven for the first time to a business because of direct-mail advertising.

- Direct mail averages an ROI of 13 to 1.

In the United States, more paper products are recovered for recycling than any other material, including plastics (8.2%), glass (27.1%), and metals (35.1%).

— U.S. Environmental Protection Agency

SUSTAINABILITY OF PRINT

A common misconception, perhaps especially among marketers, is that print is wasteful. Along with the advantage of having been manufactured from trees, a renewable resource, it is also the most recycled product in the world. The recovery rate for used paper has increased dramatically over the past decades. We recover more and know more about gaining the optimum environmental and economic benefits of using the paper we recycle.

If you've bought into the propaganda and have been objecting to including print in your marketing efforts on the basis of the environmental impact, consider these stats…

 2/24/15

- The U.S. has 20% more trees today than it did on the first Earth Day, which took place in the spring of 1970.

- Just 11% of the world's forests are used for paper (28% for lumber; 53% for fuel), according to International Paper.

- 340 lbs. of paper every year are recycled by the average person (adults and children included) and reused to create newsprint, tissue, boxboard, containerboard, and other paper products.

- A ton of paper created from recycled materials, cuts energy consumption in half and 17 trees are saved.

- Cutting-edge, eco-friendly printing technology includes copy machines that print erasable documents to be reused as blank sheets of paper and organic, vegetable-based inks, dry toners, less ink by-products, eco-friendly 3D printing, digital printing, and more.

Stats like these cannot be ignored. They clearly show that print is an eco-friendly.

Yet with 84% of U.S. adults using the internet on a daily basis, 50% owning smartphones, and tablet users doubling to 19% in 2012, according to Forrester Research, electronic campaigns will be a mainstay in the foreseeable future—but they should not stand alone.

With a multi-touch marketing campaign, you don't have to choose print or electronic (offline vs. online)—multi-touch capitalizes on the strengths of each. Let's look at how.

In 2011, nearly 53 million tons or 66.8% of the paper used in the United States was recovered for recycling, up from 33.5% in 1990. That's about 338 pounds for every adult and child in the country.

— American Forest and Paper Association

DIRECT MAIL

When you think of direct mail today, you may well have just as many negative connotations running through your mind as positive, but according to TGI, 48% of all UK adults took action as a result of receiving direct mail last year, and ExactTarget found that 65% of people who receive direct mail have made a purchase or engaged in a different marketing channel as instigated by the sender. The good news about the negative connotations is that they come primarily from marketers and that means less competition for the recipient's attention.

In August 2012, a marketing study of 353 marketers and 1,140 consumers and email-responsive adults found that 8 in 10 people open and respond to direct mail for three main reasons: The mail is from a company or a brand they know (56%); the direct mail piece is personalized (51%); and the product or service being promoted is relevant to them (44%). What's more, these reasons have remained unchanged since 2005, although the numbers have dropped slightly since their peaks.

— Marketing-Gap

Think about your own mailbox. Ten years ago, you may have received five to ten pieces of direct mail nearly every day. Today, it's likely a fraction of that. As uninformed marketers shy away from this vehicle, it simply presents itself as an even better opportunity for you and with far less noise than a recipient's email inbox—and no spam filter to block your message.

Adding direct mail to your campaign makes sense on all sorts of financial and emotional fronts. In a case study conducted by Millward Brown, he discusses the intangibles physical media such as direct mail present compared to its online counterparts. Brown asserts that physical media "leaves a deeper footprint in the brain" and produces "more brain responses connected with internal feelings, suggesting greater internalization of the ads." In other words, people respond better to something they can hold.

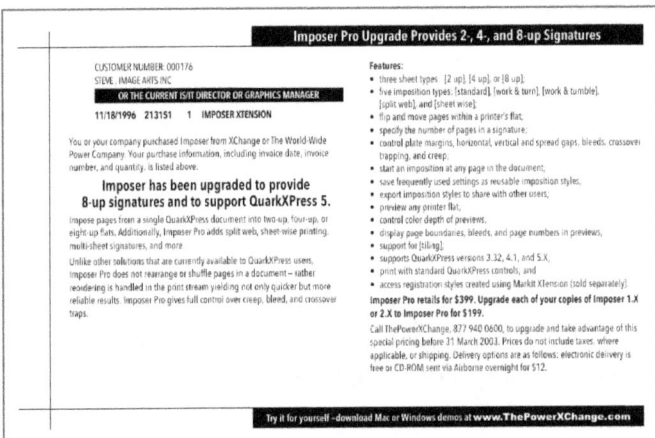

Figure 1.1 In our product-upgrade notice campaign (which we used for more than 15 years), the combination of personalization and relevance garnered us response rates as high as 85%.

PERSONALIZATION AND RELEVANCE

We, like many companies at one time, employed the shotgun approach to direct mail and often sent out as many pieces as possible, without real concern for targeting our message. This approach was seen as a lack of concern for the environment and the attitude gave direct mail a bad rap. Now, with pinpoint targeting, it's possible to send direct mail specifically and purposefully to only those that wish to receive your message and to send them a message in which they have demonstrated an interest; personalized and relevant.

Of course, the goal with direct mail, whether a postcard or envelope is to engage the recipient, but though the difference between personalization and relevance is subtle, it's important. It's one thing to greet your recipient personally, it's another thing to talk to them about a topic in which they have shown previous engagement or interest.

Beginning in the early 90s, our company produced postcards, figure 1.1 that were both. These were printed on our desktop laser printer and used to forewarn customers of an upgrade to a previous software purchase (relevance), while the greeting and purchase detail came from our invoicing system (personalization). The combination resulted in conversion rates in the 80 – 85% range.

         2/24/15

As simple as they were to produce, the postcards (or sometimes a letter format) outperformed our catalogues and more-expensive pieces many times over. With targeted messaging we also cut our postages costs by nearly half a million dollars a year. Two decades later, we're still finding better results with personalization both online and offline, and we're not alone.

According to Melissa Data, highly personalized, color, direct mail saw a 6.5% response rate, more than three times higher than the usual 2% response rate of non-personalized direct mail.

A multi-vehicle (telephone, direct mail, email) marketing research project for a large car dealership service department was conducted two years ago. The study found that customers accepted about twice as many direct mail pieces, vs. phone calls and email, before spending levels began to decline. "The researchers hypothesized that 'customers view physical mail as less intrusive than telephone calls or email—they can view such messages at their own convenience.'"

— Direct Mail

USPS EVERY DOOR DIRECT MAIL

Flying in the face of personalization comes USPS's Every Door Direct Mail® (EDDM) program, but just because you cannot personalize, does not mean a mass direct mail cannot be relevant. For many companies, your target audience really is every address, or every business address, in an area. If your business is a nail salon, lawn care provider, or grocer, you may need geo-targeting more than you need personalization. EDDM makes this possible and inexpensive.

Whether you personalize or not, according to Pitney Bowes, 76% of small business say the ideal mix includes both direct mail and electronic messaging. Developing a campaign with both online and offline components will ensure better results and evoke the emotional response that comes from simply holding a well-designed, physical piece.

Figure 1.2 In our We're Your Neighbor campaign designed for Prosper-IT, we created both an email and direct mail targeting downtown Boston businesses.

 2/24/15

FEATURE ARTICLE

In a white paper produced by CopyPress, feature articles provided the best ROI for content (inbound) marketing, and while they were not explicit in the value of an online article vs. an offline article (printed magazine, newspaper, newsletter, and the like), there's no arguing the additional real estate of a multi-page article gives you ample opportunity for details that simply cannot be captured in any other form. Even video does not offer the same stickiness a full article can provide.

The downside is, creating feature articles is also one of the most time-consuming and expensive vehicles, and for many small companies this can mean spending a large portion of your annual budget for a single product. The good news is that a feature article has legs. In fact, your feature article can be the entire focus of your multi-touch campaign by adding press releases, news announcements, a long series of social postings, and cross-promotion opportunities. Remember, with multi-touch, it's not about how many touches; it's about simultaneous touches used to firmly establish your message into the recipient's thoughts.

The takeaway here; if you can afford it, do it.

41% of Americans shop using both print catalogs and online resources.

— USPS

FLIERS, BROCHURES

Fliers and brochures have a distinct advantage in that they are great candidates for high-quality print processes, which increases the perceived value and decreases the likelihood it will find its way to the trash bin as quickly as a postcard might. What's more, there is ample room for valuable content making it relevant now and in the future.

Think carefully about how your flier or brochure can be a value-add to your multi-touch campaign. What can you include in this vehicle you cannot add elsewhere? For example, paint or color samples, scratch and sniff swatches, metallic and neon text, paper texture, and paper weight. While some of these are more intangible than others, each can increase the quality of the piece in a way digital formats cannot replicate.

40% of tourists say that tourist maps and brochures influence unplanned stops; 32% of tourists say travel brochures are the most trusted information source; and 65% of tourists used brochure display racks during their trip.

— Brochure Management

CATALOGS

Deliver magazine asserts websites supported by a catalog yield 163% more revenue than those which are not and, according to a DMA study of companies that produce a print catalog, 60% said it is their primary sales channel. Websites came in a distant second at 20%.

More importantly, catalogs have been shown to increase long-term business, which extends the effectiveness of your multi-touch campaign beyond instant gratification. 17% of people who received a catalog in the previous month purchased at least one item, compared to only 11% who received a catalog more than a month ago.

If you're looking for ideas to reduce printing costs, chat with your local print provider. Many that specialize in catalogs have co-mailing programs that can bundle your catalog with other companies' in order to reduce postage costs. These savings could be applied toward creating a higher-quality piece. Here again, think about how can you increase the value-add, now and in the future to be sure your catalog is still on the buyer's desk when they peruse your website.

Further reduction in production costs can come with simply mailing fewer catalogs. Target Marketing reports that many catalogers find online buyers buy the same amount—and sometimes more—if they are mailed fewer catalogs. Understanding to whom to send and the number to send can only come with tracking recipients and purchases. Be sure you have a thorough analytics process in place before you slash your print order. Segment your list and compare conversion rates: one set of buyers who gets frequent catalog mailings and one set of buyers who gets less-frequent mailings.

Consumers who received a retailer catalog spent 28% more on that retailer's website than consumers who did not receive a catalog.

— USPS

WHITE PAPERS

White papers share many benefits with feature articles, but require a lot less in the way of resources to produce. In fact, most experts agree your white paper should be short and to the point, but choosing a white paper will greatly depend upon your target audience. For instance, IT buyers are an ideal group and in 2009, 77% reportedly used white papers to get information about enterprise technology solutions in the previous three months.

If you're considering adding a white paper into your multi-touch campaign, consider these points:

- **Target a topic**—Your white paper cannot be all things to all readers. Choose a topic and stay focused. It's much better to be thorough on a specific topic than to touch lightly on several.

- **Start with a strong finish**—Begin with the conclusion and then use the body to traverse the thought process of your opening to your conclusion. In other words, connect the dots.

- **Think of your readers as investors**—When you approach the topic as though you want your reader to invest in the company, you can better sift out irrelevant points and stay focused.

- **Educate**—If your topic is such that you must use non-standard English, be sure to include a glossary or sidebars to introduce new topics and words with simple definitions and explanations.

- **Avoid making assumptions**—Don't assume your audience knows the material, the acronyms, or the industry jargon. Write for the general audience. Your paper may well be shared across departments—from the C-suite to the engineers, and marketing to purchasing. Make sure everyone can understand your topic.

- **Use text and graphics**—Many people scan the images in a white paper to assess the value. Others focus on the images since they are less likely to be business speak and illustrate the message more clearly. It's important to balance the two, but for many people, text only is a turnoff.

- **Be careful with length**—Consider your audience and the topic as you decide the length. While white papers can be dozens of pages long, can you really hold the interest of your audience that long? You will get much more marketing mileage from a multi-part series.

Somewhere along the way, white papers turn into ebooks and that's certainly a good vehicle as well. If you have the material and you have the audience, there's no reason not to increase the perceived value by branding your written piece as an ebook. When you do, though, you need to also consider the devices on which you are implying the document can be read and produce formats appropriate for each. An ebook should be more than just a PDF.

Direct mail campaigns should drive prospects to specific landing pages or websites where activity can be tracked and monitored.

— Aberdeen Group

PRINT ADS (INDUSTRY MAGAZINES, SHOW DIRECTORIES)

Just because you can't measure it, doesn't mean it doesn't work. Print ads often get the worst of the bad raps since the single most-concerning point of print ads is the inability to measure their effectiveness with the same degree with which we measure our site visitors or email open rates.

Circulation gives us one number for our ROI calculation, the potential audience (recipients), but measuring conversion based upon the number of people who may have seen your ad will always produce disappointing results. You need more targeted information and there are several approaches. There are four classes within the audience:

1. The number of people to whom the ad is presented (in online this is the number of impressions; in offline, the number of recipients).

2. The number of people who read the offer or content (viewers and readers).

3. The number of people to take action based upon the content's offer (click-thrus and prospects/leads [engagement]).

4. The number of people who become a customer (conversions).

To collect this offline data, you need to add events into the ad that will appeal to the different classes. For instance, if you want to track the number of people who read the ad (regardless of lead value), create an offer benefiting the casual reader—perhaps an entry into a $10,000 sweepstakes for anyone reading the ad.

If you want to track your relevant audience, you can be much less flashy. Try one of these calls to action:

- QR codes with analytics tracking

- Dedicated phone number exclusive to the ad

- Targeted landing page with analytics tracking

- Discount code with analytics and tracking for phone calls

- Sweepstakes for purchasers

- Discounts or bonus material for mentioning the ad specifically

Although these numbers still will not have the depth you get with online efforts, you will likely gain enough insight to be able to discern whether or not print ads should remain a part of your budget spend. You may be surprised.

By alternating the call to actions above, you can also determine which of the triggers rate the highest interaction and thus, improve your future print ad campaigns. This will enable you to glean information beyond recipients, readers, engagement, and conversion.

The cost per impression of an ad specialty (.6 cents) is better than that of TV (1.8 cents), magazines (1.8 cents), and newspapers (.7 cents).

CLOTHING AND TCHOTCHKES

Ad specialties span the spectrum from pens to pennants, bracelets to bumper stickers, and shirts to stockings. What you choose to brand will depend upon your budget, the campaign, your audience, and probably much more.

Tchotchkes (tradeshow baubles and giveaways) have a lasting impression hard to beat—but make it too cute and it's more likely to become a cat toy than the valuable business reminder you'd hoped.

According to the Global Advertising Specialty Impressions Study, advertising specialties have a distinct appeal to tight budgets. The cost is typically modest and the message can be perfectly tailored to the intended recipient (target audience). What's more, the cost per impression is less than that of most other forms of media and that makes it an attractive addition to any multi-touch campaign.

Knowing the likely recipient of a promotional product is paramount for an advertiser and can contribute to the low-entry cost. Branding an item with a particular appeal to target audience will mean the tchotchke is used more often and stays in use, which extends the life span and increases the number of impressions it makes. If you're not sure about that, think of the number of branded T-shirts in your closet that promote the company each time you wear it, the mouse pad on your desk that reminds you of the sponsor many times throughout the day, and that odd-shaped squeeze ball that—annoyingly—gets picked up by every single visitor to your office. Talk about stickiness and value, in the same study, 83% of people surveyed in the U.S. indicated they could identify the advertiser on a promotional item they owned.

68% of consumers believe a store's signage is reflective of the quality of its products or services.

— FedEx

POSTERS

Whether supporting your event or the main attraction (like our Creative Hell poster featured in chapter two), even in a digital world, posters remain a distinctive way to visually communicate and display information and concepts to a target audience. Posters make an ideal distribution vehicle for entertaining and informing. In our multi-touch campaign, the poster was designed like a game board to grab the attention of designers while introducing them to Lange Graphics' lenticular printing services. Using the poster as enticement, we gathered lead information from those who completed a form to receive the poster by mail. We've used infographics-style posters in much the same way. The infographic design is ideal for both online and offline distribution thus providing for a bonus vehicle in your campaign.

Technical illustrations, quick guides, education, event promotion, and so on, are just a few of the ways posters target audiences. Displayed at point-of-sale countertops, inside public events, corporate lobbies, break rooms, and the like, posters are quick bursts of information for shoppers, theatre-goers, walkers, and gawkers. If your campaign is appealing to a congregating audience of any sort, posters and signage are a must.

$5.5 billion is spent on outdoor ads each year. 62% of those outdoor ads are billboards, 15% are street furniture, 18% are bus-transit systems, and 5% are various other ads.

— Business Knowledge Source

SIGNS AND BANNERS

Signage is an inexpensive, but effective form of advertising as well, and in some cases, an essential form. You would never consider exhibiting at a show or event without signage, and there will be times when signage can and should be an offline effort within your multi-touch campaign. Signs alone can be responsible nearly entirely for drawing visitors, whether to your store, your show booth, or to a remote spot you would like them to visit.

As you develop signage to support your multi-touch campaign, there are some finer points to be considered. A quick run through this checklist will help you to design a product that is both congruent with and that supports your campaign goal.

- ✓ Is the design appropriate for the intended viewing distance?
- ✓ Is there sufficient illumination?
- ✓ Will the sign be obscured in any way?
- ✓ Is the headline short and direct enough to be read while walking or driving by?
- ✓ Is the balance of the text easily read from a distance and while moving?
- ✓ Is the sign placed conspicuously?
- ✓ Is the resolution sufficient to discernibly display the required detail of the images?
- ✓ Do the images convey messages supported by the text?
- ✓ Does the target audience have the knowledge required to understand the message?
- ✓ Did you include contact information for people too busy to stop by (e.g., dedicated phone, email, and targeted landing page to enable tracking)?
- ✓ Did you prominently feature your logo for brand awareness?

While everything on this checklist may seem obvious now, under the pressures of event coordination, it's easy to forget something important.

A single vehicle wrap can be seen up to 70,000 times in a single day.

— Cranky Creative

WRAPS

A somewhat new entry into offline-marketing options, wraps are signage adhered to (wrapped) around objects of all shapes and sizes, from boats to buses and cars to skyscrapers, wraps are seen locally 1 – 4 million times per month. A single intra-city truck with graphics is responsible for 16 million visual impressions in a year and this equates to an average cost of just 48 cents per thousand impressions.

Wraps are memorable, too. Amazingly, 80% of viewers could recall the product advertised on a vehicle wrap. According to Cox Communication/Eagle Research, 47% of 18 – 34 year olds surveyed found car wraps especially memorable. This stickiness has been responsible for as much as 107% increase in sales for some advertisers.

Wraps aren't for every campaign though, no matter how attractive the statistics. Like any other of your campaign's events, you need the right message, on the right marketing vehicle, to the right audience.

 2/24/15

COUPONS

Even though only 1% of coupons are used, in 2010, U.S. consumers redeemed 3.3 billion coupons, which reduced purchase prices about $3.7 billion. Many savvy shoppers will travel great distances to redeem a coupon and to try a new business, thus expanding your market. If they've made that type of commitment, it's clear you gain impulse purchases and cross-selling and up-selling opportunities as well. Once they are standing in your store, they often feel compelled to further justify the effort.

As a re-engagement point, studies also show coupons are effective at reactivating customers as well.

In a coupon study, consumers typically increased their purchases of items for which they received a coupon, even if they didn't use the coupon. This is referred to as *sales lift*—additional product awareness—and it's this lift that benefits your multi-touch marketing campaign when you use this offline effort.

If you're convinced coupons are for you, run through this checklist to get the most from your effort:

✓ **State a clear call to action** (CTA). Use high-performing words, such as: free, now, new, how to, save, guarantee, budget money, easy, and simple. Google's Keyword Tool is a great source of inspiration for trigger words.

✓ **Support your CTA with a strong, specific headline**. Make this a feature point of your professional design. Don't skimp. Poorly designed coupons look like they should be thrown away. Add to the perceived value with great design that includes graphics, images, and text. Make sure you include your logo for building brand awareness.

✓ Support your coupon with a **targeted landing page** or web pages describing the product and the offer.

✓ **List the benefits** to the recipient of using your product, service, or company (this is not the same as listing the features of your product).

✓ Include a small form to **capture the email address** (at a minimum) for future marketing. If feasible, also capture other contact and preferences information. The bigger the value of the coupon, the more information you can usually request in exchange.

✓ Provide **up-selling and cross-selling information**. Make sure you give them the option of getting a product that, while more expensive, might better meet their needs.

✓ **Follow up** with every redeemer.

54% of shoppers surveyed said they had already stepped up use of coupons, and even more are expected to do so.

— Wall Street Journal

ENGAGE YOUR OFFLINE VISITORS ONLINE

There are a number of paths to engaging your offline prospects and leads online. This is an important conversion when you are using offline vehicles such as those we included in the previous section. Since offline vehicles do not have the high level of engagement visibility an online vehicle offers, getting your prospect or lead to connect with you online will give you many more options for continuing advanced marketing methods.

Here are a few ideas for engaging your in-store or offline visitors in your online vehicles. Remember though, the goal is not to move offline to online and keep them there, the goal is to be able to reach your audience in the platform of their choice; and as we've shown, for many—maybe even most—their choice is print.

- **Surveys and polls**—Create an online survey or form and include the URL on purchase receipts or postcards you hand out.

- **Sign-up list**—Keep a sign-up sheet near your cash register so your customers can add their name to a subscribers' list.

- **Contests**—Sponsor a contest and provide the URL in ads and at your store so your customers can enter.

- **Coupons and promotions**—Promote web-only specials and coupons in point-of-sale material and offline marketing vehicles, available only upon enrollment at your website.

- **Add a QR (quick response) code (a two-dimensional graphical code)**—These special codes can be read by many smartphones directing users to targeted landing pages, your social-media network, or sign-up forms.

When evaluating the success of your multi-touch (or multi-channel) campaigns, it's important to look past the last touch point when attributing conversion credit. Here it's the accumulative benefit of the many touch points that account for the conversion.

 2/24/15

CHAPTER 2: MULTI-TOUCH MARKETING

According to Pitney Bowes, 76% of small businesses state their ideal marketing mix is a combination of print and digital communications. Whether you call this mix multi-touch, multi-channel, multi-vehicle, or cross-media marketing, it is a strategy that parlays the strengths of multiple marketing vehicles to more quickly and successfully guide the prospect through the purchasing process.

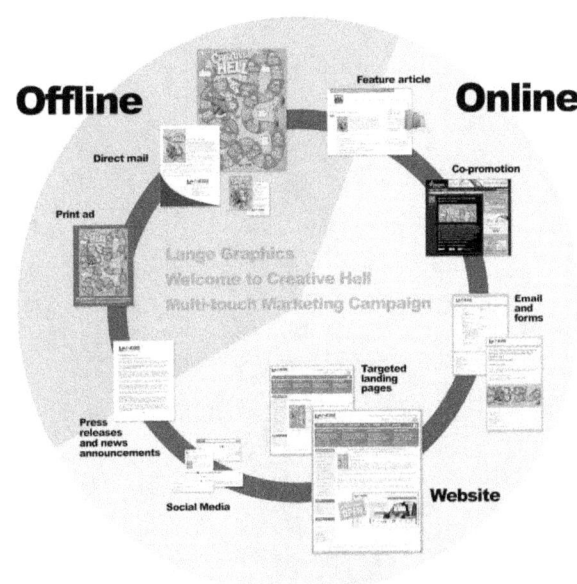

Figure 2.1 Lange Graphics' multi-touch campaign included several online and offline vehicles.

A recent example of a multi-touch campaign we created is the Lange Graphics Creative Hell campaign shown in figure 2.1. Welcome to Creative Hell is the epitome of the power of print.

The goal was to acquire customers for Lange Graphics' lenticular printing services and we felt the tipping point of lenticular is when the client holds it and, for 3D, see it in action. That meant we needed to put a vibrant sample in the recipient's hand; but because of the expense of lenticular, we needed a way to target the audience carefully.

In this campaign, print was not just the pivotal moment, it was foundation for the entire project and it gave us an opportunity to reach marketing directors and remind them how important print is—and can be for their clients.

The Creative Hell multi-touch campaign featured first and foremost a large poster with specific appeal for our identified target audience: marketing directors who make decisions about which vehicles are used within their clients' campaigns.

         2/24/15

The call-to-action offer was to complete a form to receive a full-sized, printed wall poster poking fun at the challenges we marketers and designers face every day. Through humor, we aimed to acquire the attention of marketers who would complete the form with full contact information in order to receive the poster by mail. The poster, a fine example of Lange Graphics' offset print capabilities, also included a digitally printed and welcoming introduction letter further detailing their services.

As requests came in, recipients were evaluated based upon their job title, and if our criteria met, in addition to the full-sized poster, Lange Graphics sent along a small 3D postcard that showed the eye-catching features of lenticular. See figure 2.2.

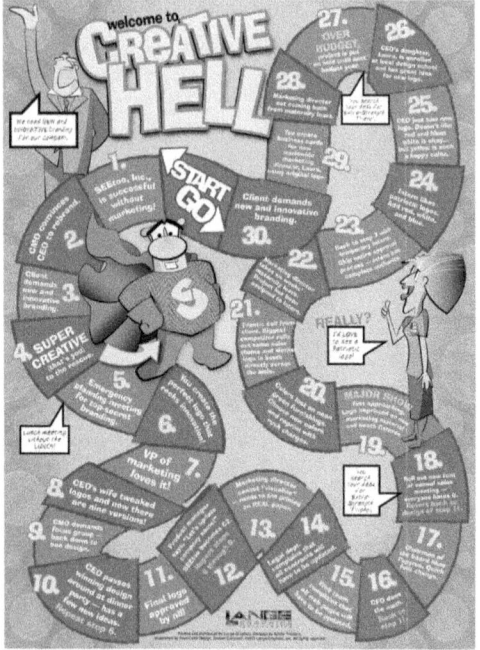

Figure 2.2 We used this full-sized, colorful poster to entice the marketer to provide their contact information in order to receive the poster by mail. Since we wanted to acquire both mailing addresses and email addresses, creating a piece that required shipment, enabled us to meet this goal.

Figure 2.3 If the recipient was not marketing director or similar role, they received only the poster and the welcome letter shown above.

Figure 2.4 If our criteria were met, the subscriber also received a small, two-sided 3D postcard that beautifully featured the unique nature of lenticular printing.

With our multi-touch campaign, we were able to reach our target audience through a number of offline and online vehicles, including:

- direct mail

- email

- press releases and news announcements

- targeted landing pages

- in-site article

- home-page feature

- social-media postings

- co-promotion offers

- third-party online and offline feature articles

- social-media postings

- online directory listings

This particular mix of online and offline was chosen based upon a number of factors: message, audience, available lists, ability to segment, budget, cost of production, estimated ROI, and recipient reception. Some campaigns are best serviced using as few as two vehicles, but your expectations should be the same: make your message more sticky through repetition.

Multi-touch marketing—A series of selling campaigns intended to reach a target audience with a consistent message that is carried over a variety of vehicles to reinforce a company's brand and message. By using a multi-touch approach, companies make it convenient for customers to receive and respond in whatever manner is preferred.

CHAPTER 3: MARKETING VEHICLES

There are dozens of marketing vehicles that will generate leads and contacts, enable you to reach your leads and prospects (and advance their sales readiness), and even to sell to leads and prospects, converting them into customers. Our list is but a snapshot, but ideally it will get your creative juices flowing so you can customize a multi-touch event of your own.

INBOUND VS. OUTBOUND

Hierarchically, we divide marketing first as inbound and outbound content, then secondarily as online and offline. A robust multi-touch campaign may well include several to many vehicles within these categories.

The act of sending your message out or broadcasting your message is the easy definition of outbound marketing. With outbound marketing you are *asking for the business*. This can include TV, print ads, cold calling, outside sales, tradeshow exhibiting, and email. With most traditional outbound marketing, it can be difficult or impossible to track results: how many people saw your commercial, heard your radio ad, or saw you at a tradeshow? This is seen as a downside for many, but as we discussed earlier, there are ways you can engage your offline audience online and gain tracking ability and visibility.

In order to bolster outbound results, smart companies turn to inbound marketing as well; this includes social media, downloadable resources, and other types of engagement where you are *earning the business*. With inbound marketing, you drive people to seek out your product and educate them on the benefits of your offerings and thus, win the business. With inbound, you are reaching people who are already, perhaps, searching for or at least interested in learning about your product specifically or products like yours.

Outbound marketing is about interruption. Inbound marketing is about discovery.

— B2B Digital Marketing

ONLINE VS. OFFLINE

Smart marketers deploy both online and offline vehicles. They know that in order to extend their reach to all possible niches in which their clients congregate, they need to meet them on their own turf. Online, of course, means your website, social media, email, targeted landing pages, and other digital representations, while offline includes direct mail, tradeshows, direct sales, call centers, and the like.

While there is no standard set of vehicles you should deploy, there are common choices. Your message and your audience will influence which vehicles are best for your campaign. Online vehicles make up your digital footprint, whether it's your website, a social-media site, an email inbox, or a peer's blog.

WEBSITE

The foundation for your marketing efforts will always be your website. Even if your campaign is primarily print-based, you would be remiss to omit at least a reference to your website and specifically to a targeted landing page (for tracking). It is critical your website support your marketing message. If you are marketing a new widget, you can be sure that the recipient of your campaign will look to verify it at your website and you need to meet that expectation.

Pages within your website can be used to provide your customers with information beyond that which will fit within the design constraints of your printed piece. You can also augment the message in a way not possible with printed vehicles, by providing links to digital resources such as downloads or multimedia.

Think of your website as your 24/7 sales team. No matter where or when your recipient receives any one of your marketing vehicles, more information is a click away. Use this real estate wisely and thoroughly.

One of the commonly accepted website traffic theories is that visitors tend to come back 5 to 7 times before they buy

— Dewpointe

TARGETED LANDING PAGES

Targeted landing pages are individual web pages within your site providing dedicated space to drive your message home—whether your originating message was outbound, inbound, offline, or online. It's very important your targeted landing page matches the design of the marketing vehicle that drove the visit and that you specifically welcome the visitor.

For instance, if your Twitter account is the marketing vehicle, create a landing page with a greeting at the top welcoming Twitter followers; likewise for other social accounts or mentions. This targeted landing page has three primary benefits:

- Visitors feel special when you welcome them specifically.

- When you associate the originating source for each page's traffic individually, it enables you to track the number of visits (and other analytics) more easily.

- You can test the effectiveness of specific components within the pages to see what messaging, design, or elements contribute to improved conversion rates.

A targeted landing page might contain text only, a form, video, links to downloadable resources, testimonials, or any other information that you believe will advance the recipient's sales readiness.

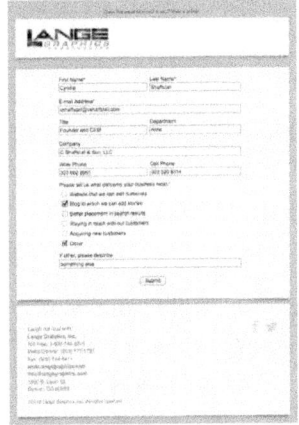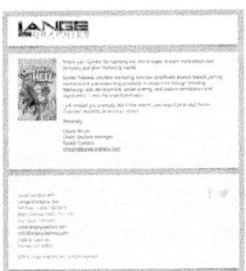

Figure 3.1 This targeted landing page contains a form, social follow icons, and contact information. When the form is submitted, an automatic email is sent that thanks the subscriber for their submission. In that email, also shown, we further engage the recipient with links to the Lange Graphics' website. The purpose of the landing page is to get them to fill out the form, so we try to keep distractions to a minimum.

When designing a targeted landing page, run through this checklist for best results:

✓ Be polite, welcome the visitor, and say thank you.

✓ Use a design consistent with the other event components.

✓ Start with a strong, appealing headline and subheads.

✓ Provide a graphical, clear call-to-action button to indicate what they should do (click now, watch the video, buy now, and so on).

✓ Remember your page is about the visitor so answer their questions quickly and tell them what you can do for them.

✓ Talk about benefits (what's in it for them), not features.

✓ Make sure your pitch contains a clear value proposition.

✓ Close the page with who you are, how to contact you, and how they can learn more about you.

✓ If appropriate, add a link to your privacy policy to lessen their concern about filling out forms.

A *microsite* is a collection of targeted landing pages used to support a marketing vehicle and often made up of duplicates of other pages at your site. Microsites disseminate information beyond what can be included in a single landing page. With the addition of a navigational menu, you can closely mimic the layout, design, and functionality of the full site while staying design consistent with your marketing vehicle in a set of pages for a captive audience. This subset of your site's pages will help you to better understand the visitor's needs and behavior.

Lead nurturing. A systematic approach to developing new leads into sales-qualified leads—or in other words, warming cold leads to hot leads. Emails are sent consecutively and with the purpose of nurturing the recipient along the path to purchase.

                        2/24/15

ONLINE MULTI-TOUCH VEHICLES

TRIGGERED MARKETING (JUST-IN-TIME MARKETING)

To create your own multi-touch marketing campaign, you'll want to use every vehicle that makes sense in achieving your goal. Your multi-touch campaign can effectively be used to launch a new marketing initiative and, to that end, also include a triggered campaign in the form of either a drip campaign or a nurturing campaign.

Marketing automation enables you to be in front of your client with the right offer at the right time. With triggered campaigns, you transcend from *when-you-can marketing* to *just-in-time marketing* and it makes a difference. Said in another way, with marketing automation, you reach your leads and prospects at a time most relevant to them rather than when it's most convenient for you.

website	Wikipedia	online marketplaces	opinion and review sites
mobile apps	online display/text ads	multimedia resources	SMS (text messaging)
opinion and review sites	email	social news	online feature articles
social media	social bookmarking	surveys	downloadable resources
targeted landing page	press releases	in-app ads	co-promotion

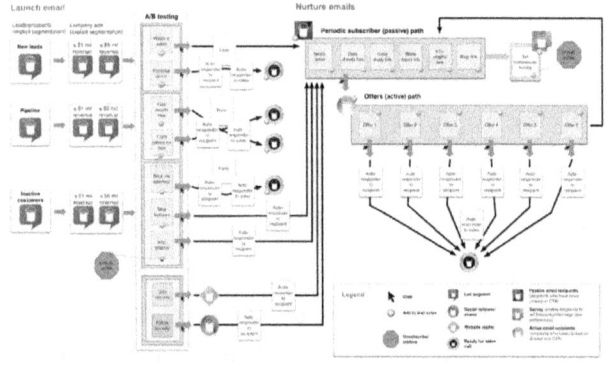

Figure 3.2 Nurturing campaigns can be launched independently or embedded within a multi-touch marketing campaign. If you use auto-responder emails at all, whether as part of a multi-touch campaign or a single-event campaign, it is technically categorized as a nurturing campaign.

These automated campaigns become targeted with the application of explicit and implicit data. This will also help you to make great strides in:

- Response rates
- Cross-sell and up-sell activity
- Relevance of messaging and offers
- Timeliness of delivery

 2/24/15

A client may take days, weeks, months, or even years to make a purchasing decision and you need to be at the forefront of their thoughts at the critical moment. A multi-touch campaign typically deploys all marketing components to the various vehicles at or around the same time, but by including a triggered campaign under the multi-touch umbrella you have an automated approach to sending appropriate marketing responses to your prospects' actions or interactions as they occur and over any time span. It effectively extends the campaign and moves you toward just-in-time marketing.

Technological advancements in software have made event-triggered marketing an indispensable component of marketing strategies. Triggered campaigns typically require less effort than a string of one-off emails, but there is an up-front expense in both time and resources to be managed. Start by mapping out well-defined goals for both your new and existing target audiences and include the C-suite, upper management, and sales team in developing triggers, conversions, and ROI measurements.

Triggered campaigns are challenging at best and though they share many of the same requirements as single-event campaigns, they have moving parts that far outnumber most other types of events. With that said, it's easy to feel overwhelmed no matter how much staff or experience you have.

The top three channels used for lead nurturing are: email 65%, phone calls 44%, and direct mail 25%.

— Aberdeen Group

NURTURE MARKETING

A nurturing campaign is made up of multiple components designed to develop leads as sales ready. The process is used to build relationships and develop trust with prospects in a way that is both consistent and relevant. A schematic is used to visually map out your strategy, rules, and responses—and to act as a map for the building of your creatives and triggered events. This event shown in figure 3.2, provides for basic segmentation of the lists, testing of launch email messages, confirmation email, and a series of nurturing emails for recipients learn about the program (recipients are *graduated* from the program if they complete the contact form at any stage).

A lead-nurturing funnel consists of multiple touches using more than one marketing vehicle, all geared toward achieving a particular marketing goal. The effort could start with the goal of generating leads by having prospects fill out online web forms. To start this process, the funnel begins with emails that are sent out with a specific call to action. When a prospect fills out a web form, and the lead is generated, a series of emails is sent to then nurture the lead along the sales path. When direct mail is added to that marketing mix—such as a handwritten note, a discount offer, or direct mail—the likelihood of a winning campaign increases exponentially.

The benefits of drip marketing include: building top-of-mind awareness, cultivating relationships, good will and trust, creating preference for your brand, and increasing your rate of conversion over time.

— DMN3

DRIP MARKETING

Like nurturing, drip marketing is a campaign strategy where messaging to your prospects, clients, or customers is also sent over a span of time. These are intentionally spaced to act as reminders, like a drip-irrigation system keeping your garden watered.

Drip marketing can be as simple as sending a weekly email, a monthly newsletter, or a regular discount coupon. The drips don't have to be in the same format either. Any type of messaging will do. Since most products and services have a sales span, the idea is to keep the messaging in front of your contacts until the point they are ready to engage or make a purchase. Unlike nurturing, drip is more about building trust and relationships so the recipient thinks of you first when their need for your product or services finally matures or presents itself.

As you develop a self-promotion marketing initiative, you may want to incorporate drip marketing or a nurturing campaign—a long-term approach to keeping your company in front of potential clients.

Drip campaigns are delivered based on pre-determined time intervals while triggered marketing campaigns are initiated based on prospect behavior.

— Ian Michaels, Customer Think

 2/24/15

CHAPTER 4: MULTI-TOUCH PLANNING

It's quite easy for a multi-touch campaign to become unwieldy, especially when you embed a multi-event nurturing or drip campaign. We recommend you map your program using a schematic of some sort. Our application of choice is OmniGraffle®, but you can use Excel®, PowerPoint®, or any drawing application that allows you illustrate the steps for tracking and planning, what information will be gathered, and how it will be used.

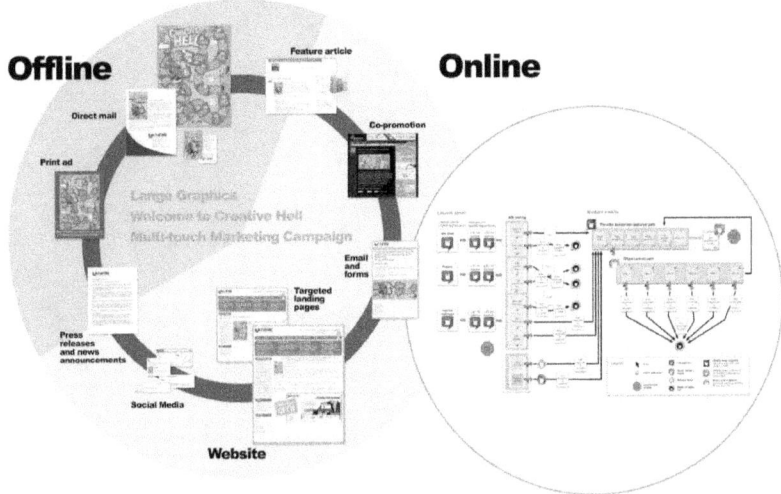

Figure 4.1 In this schematic you can see an example of how you could embed a nurturing campaign into a multi-touch campaign.

This schematic merges the nurturing campaign shown in chapter three with our multi-touch campaign of chapter two. It makes sense to merge them. As we collect the contact information of our target audience through our multi-touch efforts, we add the engaged names into a new list (bucket) where they will receive a welcome email and become a member of our long-term nurturing or drip campaign. In this way, whether or not they choose to purchase lenticular services immediately, we will remind them of Lange Graphics' services regularly or provide them with other valuable content (videos, slide decks, paper samples, newsletters, coupons, and so on), in order to keep them engaged with the client's brand.

When you think of these extended campaigns, liken them to a pinball in play and imagine yourself tallying the points each time you connect with a bumper, slingshot, target, or flipper (lead/prospect). Keep the ball in play as long as possible and learn from your errors, correct your strategy, and come back to rack up the high score. This is an apropos analogy for multi-touch marketing.

According to recent studies by the Direct Marketing Association and the U.S. Postal Service: the average consumer receives 25 pieces of domestic mail per week; the number of companies sending 500,000+ marketing emails more than doubled in two years, from 21% in 2002 to 51% in 2004; and 55% of postal mail recipients look forward to discovering the mail each day.

— DMN3

 2/24/15

CHAPTER 5: CONCLUSION

Getting your name out there is critical to building and maintaining your brand and establishing a good professional reputation. Regular distribution of marketing vehicles—of both the online and offline variety—will help in this process as clients come to learn about your company, products, or services. Marketing vehicles can also be used to establish your company as an authority and a trusted advisor and to be in front of your client when the time comes for them to make a purchasing decision.

We've all read the stats that email marketing is the most-used and cost-effective method to nurture leads, but the importance of direct mail should not be underestimated. A campaign that combines the delivery of electronic mail with print represents a best-in-class multi-touch campaign with a WOW! factor gives your message measurable stickiness.

Spider Trainers has particular expertise in print and has conducted hundreds of multi-touch campaigns and sent millions of direct-mail pieces and emails on behalf of its clients and internal use. We test, track, and tweak campaigns to gather the knowledge required to achieve true ROI—for many companies that's the true definition of conversion.

Triggered campaigns, traditional email sends, and direct-mail marketing combined with the other vehicles offer results that are impressive, but because of all these moving parts, multi-touch campaigns can seem overwhelming. While it is our hope we have provided you with plenty of in-depth information about how you can get started, if you still don't feel comfortable, consider hiring outside help. Once you have your first campaign going, you'll be on your way to effectively reaching your clients, getting them to engage, and meeting your goals.

Even among the most connected consumers, new-product discovery largely happens offline via sources such as word-of-mouth, direct mail, catalogs, and television.

— IAB

REFERENCES AND CREDITS

ASI Central: Global Advertising Specialties Impressions Study

http://www.asicentral.com/asp/open/Research/impressionsstudy/Ad_Spec_Impressions_Study_2010.pdf

B2B Digital: Inbound Marketing vs. Outbound Marketing: The Difference is Friction

http://b2bdigital.net/2012/10/16/inbound-marketing-vs-outbound-marketing-the-difference-is-friction/

Brochure Management

http://www.brochuremanagement.com/index.php?/Brochure-Marketing/brochure-marketing.html

Business Knowledge Source: Using Billboards for Marketing

http://www.businessknowledgesource.com/marketing/using_billboards_for_marketing_026351.html

Content Marketing Institute: Aberdeen Lead Nurturing Study

http://www.contentmarketinginstitute.com/wp-content/uploads/2012/07/Aberdeen-Lead-Nurturing-study.pdf
http://contentmarketinginstitute.com/2011/12/2012-b2b-content-marketing-research/

CopyPress

http://www.copypress.com/White_Paper.pdf

Cranky Creative

http://www.crankycreative.com/faq/vehicle-wrap-stats/

Customer Think: Drip Marketing vs. Trigger Marketing Campaigns. Is One Better Than the Other?

http://www.customerthink.com/blog/drip_marketing_vs_trigger_marketing_campaigns_is_one_better_than_the_other

DaNite Sign Company: Importance of Signs

http://www.danitesign.com/pdfs/Importance-of-Signs.pdf

Dewpointe: Does the Average Website Visitor Return 7 Times Before They Buy

http://www.dewpointe.com/business-coaching-corner/does-the-average-website-visitor-return-7-times-before-they-buy/

Effectiveness of Print Advertising

http://www.prnewswire.com/news-releases/effectiveness-of-print-advertising-176449041.html

eMarketer: Which Marketing Tactics Have the Best ROI?

http://www.emarketer.com/Article/Which-Content-Marketing-Tactics-Best-ROI/1009706

ExactTarget: 4 Glaring Statistics You Need to Know About Direct Mail Marketing

http://www.business2community.com/marketing/4-glaring-statistics-you-need-to-know-about-direct-mail-marketing-0294347

fast.MAP: The 8th gast.MAP Marketing GAP PDF

http://www.fastmap.com/whitepapers/pdfs/The-8th-fast.MAP-Marketing-GAP-PDF.pdf

FedEx: Office of the Times Survey

http://news.van.fedex.com/fedex-office-survey-standout-signs-contribute-sales

IAB: The Multiscreen Marketer

http://www.iab.net/multiscreenmarketer

Journal of Marketing

http://www.journals.marketingpower.com/doi/abs/10.1509/jmkg.75.4.94

Kessler Creative: What is Multi-touch Marketing?

http://www.kesslercreative.com/blog/index.php/what-is-multi-touch-marketing/

MarketingSherpa: Lead Nurturing: 3-part Funnel Campaign Creates 70% Increase in Inbound Calls to Sales Reps Case Study

http://www.marketingsherpa.com/article/case-study/3part-funnel-campaign-creates-70

Melissa Data: The Effectiveness of Highly Personalized Direct Mail

http://www.melissadata.com/newsreleases/effectiveness-of-highly-personalized-direct-mail.htm

Millward Brown Case Study

http://www.millwardbrown.com/Libraries/MB_Case_Studies_Downloads/MillwardBrown_CaseStudy_Neuroscience.sflb.ashx

Pitney Bowes

http://www.pitneybowes.com

Print in the Mix: Drip Marketing: Consumer Dialog that Builds Preference—DMN3

http://printinthemix.com/Fastfacts/Show/566

Target Marketing Magazine: 9 Reasons to Reconsider Catalog Direct Mail

http://www.targetmarketingmag.com/article/9-reasons-reconsider-catalog-classic-direct-mail-piece/2

TechCrunch: Forrester: 84% Of U.S. Adults Now Use The Web Daily, 50% Own Smartphones, Tablet Ownership Doubled To 19% In 2012

http://techcrunch.com/2012/12/19/forrester-84-of-u-s-adults-now-use-the-web-daily-50-own-smartphones-tablet-ownership-doubled-to-19-in-2012/

The More You Know B&B: Direct Mail Statistics You Can't Ignore

http://themoreyouknowbandb.wordpress.com/2012/11/11/4-direct-mail-statistics-you-cant-ignore/

USPS: Direct Mail: A natural for building stronger online sales

https://www.usps.com/business/pdf/comScore_Retail_WP.pdf

Value of Print: The Value of Print Flipbook

http://value.printing.org/page/10574

.

2/24/15

ABOUT SPIDER TRAINERS

Spider Trainers provides multi-touch online and offline marketing and web development to make your brand more visible, elevate search-engine rankings, attract appropriate visitors, and enable educated purchasing decisions.

Spider Trainers has created a process for marketing initiatives that provides optimization for your product, services, and company, and, through the exposure of your executive staff's professional accomplishments, also builds validating information to provide additional search-engine lift.

Spider Trainers has decades of experience in print, web development, go-to-market initiatives, and sustainable, behavior-based (online and offline), traditional and emerging marketing strategies.

For more information about our company, visit www.spidertrainers.com

SPECIALTIES

- online and offline multi-touch marketing
- multi-event drip and nurturing campaigns
- search-engine optimization
- web development (including mobile)
- ad and campaign design and deployment

SPIDER TRAINERS CONTACT

Phone: 651 702 3793
Email: spidertrainer@spidertrainers.com
Website: http://www.spidertrainers.com

Address: PO Box 280487
Lakewood, CO 80228 United States